ANIMAL LAFFS

by

MURRAY LORING

and

SEYMOUR GLASOFER

Illustrated by

ALEX BLOCH

 JONATHAN DAVID PUBLISHERS, INC.
MIDDLE VILLAGE, NEW YORK 11379

ANIMALAFFS
by Murray Loring & Seymour Glasofer

Copyright © 1982
by Jonathan David Publishers, Inc.

Address all inquiries to:
Jonathan David Publishers, Inc.
68-22 Eliot Avenue
Middle Village, New York 11379

10 9 8 7 6 5 4 3 2 1

Library of Congress Cataloging in Publication Data

Loring, Murray
Animalaffs.

   1. Animals—Anecdotes, facetiae, satire, etc. I. Glasofer,
Seymour, 1921— II. Title.
PN6231.A5L65 1982   818'.5402   82-9985
ISBN 0-8246-0287-0   AACR2

Printed in the United States of America

In Gratitude

This book could not have been
written without the collaboration
of our dedicated wives,
Mimi Loring
and
Lillian Glasofer

HIGH ON MILK

On bumper of farmer's truck: GET HIGH ON MILK; MY COWS ARE ALL ON GRASS.

READY, SET, SHOOT

A skunk family was cornered by a pack of wolves. The mama skunk turned to her babies and said, "Let us spray."

THE BULL SOUND

Watch out for little old ladies! Last week one of them came up to the after-dinner speaker and said, "Sir, you may find this hard to believe, but your speech reminded me of a little dog I have at home."

"Isn't that sweet," said the speaker. "Imagine! My speech reminded you of a little dog you have at home! What kind of dog do you have?"

"Bull!" she answered.

CURRENTLY UNHAPPY

The poor electric eel was sitting sadly in the aquarium. "What's the matter?" asked the custodian.

"I'm unhappy because I have no wife," replied the eel.

The custodian ordered another eel, but still the first eel continued to brood. "What's the matter now?" asked the custodian.

"Dammit!" the eel replied, pointing toward his intended mate: "D.C."

ELEPHANT TRICKS

"That's a werry knowin' hannimal of yours," said a Cockney gentleman to the keeper of an elephant.

"Very," was the cool rejoinder.

"It performs strange tricks and hantics, does he?" inquired the Cockney, eyeing the animal.

"Yes," retorted the keeper, "we've even learned him to put money in that box you see up there. Try him with a crown."

The Cockney handed the elephant a crown piece; and, sure enough, he took it in his trunk and then placed it in the box, high out of reach.

"Well, that is wherry hextraordinary-hastonishing,

truly," said the visitor. "Now let's see him take it out, and hand it back to me."

"We never learnt him that trick," retorted the keeper smugly.

*   *   *

When the baby gorilla was born at the Toledo Zoo, a sign was placed on the cage: IT'S A GIRLILLA!

PAYING THE POOPER

The hipster's dog got loose and ran away from the jam session. He noticed a parking meter by the curb, and was about to approach it when a motorist slipped a dime into the slot.

"Man!" said the bopster dog as he flipped. "Dig that crazy pay toilet!"

MOSQUITO PROBLEM

Two mosquitos were cruising along a super-highway one day, and one said to the other: "Look down there. It's Dean Martin!"

Replied the other: "You bite him. I'm driving."

TRYING TO SKIN A KATZ

While bargain-hunting for things to add to her collection of rare bric-a-brac, Josephine Rockefeller stopped one day at the little curio shop of Sam Katz. Finding nothing of interest, she was about to leave when, just inside the door, she noticed a cat lapping milk out of a saucer. After one glance she realized that the saucer was a priceless antique.

Hoping that Sam was unaware of the saucer's value she said, "That's a nice cat you have there, Sam. Would you sell him to me?"

Well," said Sam, "I'd be willing to sell him for five dollars, I guess."

Josephine paid the proprietor and put the cat under her arm. "By the way" she added casually, "I suppose you won't mind if I just take the saucer along. The cat is probably used to eating from it."

"Oh, no," said Sam, "I can't give you the saucer."

"That's ridiculous, Sam. Why not!" protested Mrs. Rockefeller.

"Because," said Sam, "from that old saucer, I already sold 139 cats."

LAMENT OF A PIG

A pig was lamenting to a cow about how unpopular he was. "Everyone talks about your gentleness," said the pig. "You give milk and cream, but I give so much more: I give ham, bacon, bristles, and my feet are pickled, yet nobody likes me. I can't understand why?"

The cow considered this question and then answered, "Well, maybe it's because I give while I'm still living."

JUST CHECKING

1st Hunter: "Hey, Bill."
2nd Hunter: "Yeah."
1st Hunter: "Are you all right?"
2nd Hunter: "Yeah."
1st Hunter: "Then, I shot a bear."

A CASUAL VISITOR

George Murphy answered the doorbell and admitted a friend and the huge dog that trailed behind. As the two men talked, the dog knocked over a lamp, jumped on the sofa, and began chewing one of the cushions.

Unable to contain himself, George growled, "Can't you do something to make your dog behave?"

"My dog!" exclaimed the friend. "I thought it was your dog."

* * *

What did the young doe say as she ran from the woods?

"That's the last time I do it for two bucks."

TO MAKE A POINT

"Uncle" Joe Cannon, the late speaker of the House, was once telling Chauncey Depew, in somewhat exaggerated terms, about a fish he had nearly caught.

"About the size of a whale, was it?" asked Depew.

"I was baitin' with whales," said "Uncle" Joe.

BOSSIE, SUSIE, AND BUTTERCUP

A journalism graduate got his first job as a reporter on a country weekly. The managing editor was quick to impress upon him that every detail, including names, be included in every news story.

The first story handed in by the young reporter read: "Last night during a severe electrical storm, lightning killed three cows on a farm south of town. Their names were Bossie, Susie, and Buttercup."

A TIME FOR PATIENCE

A man who sits in a swamp all day waiting to shoot a duck will complain if his wife has dinner ten minutes late.

TOO MUCH PULL

A man visiting a pet shop noticed a parrot with a string tied to each leg. "What are the strings for?" he asked.

"Pull one and see," the attendant said.

He pulled the string on the right leg, and the parrot said, "Hello there."

Then he pulled the string on the left leg, and the bird said. "Pleased to meet you."

"What would happen if I pulled both strings at once?" the man asked.

"I'd fall on my tail, you dummy!" croaked the parrot.

VETS TAKE NOTE

Important memo to veterinarians: If you receive a call to examine a mustang, cougar, or jaguar, be sure the caller isn't trying to reach a mechanic.

SMART HORSE

Farmer: "This horse is as smart as I am!"

Vet: "Don't tell anyone. You may want to sell him one day."

WHEN A PARROT IS INSULTED

Alex had been trying to teach his new parrot to talk, and every day for several months he greeted it with "Good morning!" But the parrot never responded.

One morning Alex walked past the bird, ignoring him completely.

"Hey, what's the matter with you this morning?" shouted the parrot.

OUTWITTING A FISH CLERK

A lady was browsing about the pet shop looking at the fish in the tanks. "Mister," she addressed the clerk, "how much are the goldfish?"

"They're two for twenty-nine cents," said the clerk.

"How much is that one?" asked the lady.

"That one, Ma'am, is fifteen cents," replied the clerk.

"Give me the other one," said the lady.

UNRIPE CANARIES

"Mommy," exclaimed the child upon seeing some green parakeets in a pet shop, "here are some canaries that aren't ripe yet!"

BOUNDING AND A-BUTTING

Angry man: "Why did you tax me eight dollars for my goat?"

Tax adjuster: "Well, then, just keep him off the street. The laws says, 'For private possessions bounding and a-butting on public property, two dollars a running foot.'"

PESSIMISTS & OPTIMISTS

One of Ronald Reagan's favorite animal stories is about two boys—one an optimist, the other a pessimist.

The pessimist was left in a large room full of wonderful and exciting toys. The optimist was left in a room full of manure.

When the door of the pessimist was opened, there stood the boy crying and apprehensive, worrying that someone would take away his toys.

When the door of the optimist was opened, there he was busy shoveling away the manure like there was no tomorrow, first over one shoulder, then over the other.

"Why are you working so hard?" a neighbor asked.

"There's gotta be a pony in there somewhere," he responded.

HORSE BETS

"I want a two dollar ticket on myself," said the horse, as he approached the pari-mutuel window.

"What?" exclaimed the ticket seller.

"Shocked that I can talk?" asked the horse.

"No. I just don't think you can win."

AN UNDER-EDUCATED PARROT

A certain lady who lived on Park Avenue loved birds. Her husband was rich and he indulged her every whim. For a birthday present, he located and sent her a parrot that spoke eleven languages. The cost: exactly one hundred dollars for each language.

"What d'ya think of that wonderful bird I sent you, dear?"

"It certainly was elegant," she answered. "It's in the oven right now."

The husband's face turned purple.

"In the oven?" he shouted. "Why, that bird could speak eleven languages."

"Then why didn't it say something?" protested the wife.

PARAKEET-POSTURE

In a pet shop one parakeet lay on his back, one foot hooked oddly into the cage wire. A customer was about to alert the saleswoman to the bird's plight when he noticed a sign taped to the cage:

No, I am not sick.

No, I am not dead.

No, my leg is not stuck in the cage.

I just like to sleep this way.

SUPER-STORK

Army paratroopers were practicing their jumps in a backwoods region near the home of a mountaineer with fifteen children. One of the youngsters saw the parachute floating down with a man attached to it, and ran into the house yelling, "Bring your shotgun, pappy! The stork is bringin' 'em full-grown now!"

BIRDS AND BEES AND CENTIPEDES

A mama centipede took her young daughter aside one day to tell her about the "birds and the bees" and the facts of life, and how to avoid unwelcome male centipedes.

The youngster listened intently and finally spoke up. "But mama dear, which legs do I cross?"

THE FARMER'S MOTHER-IN-LAW
AND THE MULE

A mule once kicked a farmer's mother-in-law to death. A tremendous crowd gathered for the funeral, and strangely, most of the people were men. "This old lady must certainly have been very popular," said the minister to the farmer. Look at all the people who left their work to come to her funeral!"

"They're not here for the funeral," observed one of those who had come. "They're here to buy the mule."

* * *

Baby bird to mother bird: "You're not just going to push me out without any flight instructions?"

BIRDS & BEES & GIRLS & GUYS

"Who made me?" asked the Little Bee
One morning of his ma.
"It's pretty clear the time is ripe
For me to learn the facts of life
From either you or pa.

"And ma, I want to know the truth
For I'm too old for toys,
And frankly, I've begun to doubt
Those silly fairy tales about
The little girls and boys."

A PEKINGESE BITCH

A gentle little lady who had been watching the antics of a Pekingese in the pet shop window came in to price it.

"That bitch," said the salesman. "You can have it for thirty dollars."

The lady winced. "What's the matter?" asked the salesman. "Aren't you familiar with the term 'bitch'?"

"Yes," she said, "But I never before heard it applied to a dog."

READING A CHICKEN HIS RIGHTS

An elderly city dweller moved to the country and decided to raise poultry. Never having lived on a farm before he relied heavily on books, pamphlets, and the advice of a friendly farmer who lived close by.

When the time came to kill his first chicken, he rounded up the victim and tucked it under his arm along with a book on poultry processing. Behind the barn, still holding the chicken under his arm, he began reading up on procedure. Finally, he put down the book, and as he looked up he found his neighbor studying the scene. For a moment, the friendly farmer didn't say anything. Then, with a slight smile spreading on his face, he asked, "Reading him his rights are you?"

A FEELING OF INADEQUACY

Two cows were grazing near the highway when a milk distribution truck passed by with lettering on its side that read:
"PASTEURIZED, HOMOGENIZED,
VITAMINS A & D ADDED."
One cow turned to the other and said, "Makes me feel kind of inadequate. How about you?"

A BAD START

A young attorney was trying his first case. A farmer had engaged him to sue a veterinarian for the loss of 24 pigs. Attempting to impress the jury with the magnitude of the loss, the young lawyer shouted, "Twenty-four pigs! Twenty-four! Think of that! Twice the number in the jury box!"

THE HORSE YOU BACKED CALLED

Husband and wife were having breakfast.

"You had a very restless night, dear," said the wife, "and what's more you kept murmuring a woman's name in your sleep. Now, tell me, who is Daisy?"

"Oh-er," he stammered, "the fact is, my dear, Daisy is the name of a filly I backed yesterday. It won, 10-to-1, and here's your share."

Handing his wife a five-dollar bill, he picked up the morning newspaper and hid himself behind it.

In the evening, at the dinner table, his wife pursued the subject.

"By the way," she said, "you know that horse you backed yesterday? Well, she telephoned this afternoon."

PAP'S BLUE RIBBON

A Scotch terrier took his wife and puppy to see a dog show and promptly was pulled out of the audience to receive the blue ribbon awarded for first prize in his class. Startled and gratified, on the way home the Scottie stopped off at a tavern to celebrate his good fortune. When he got home he discovered that he had left the prize on the bar and he sent the puppy to retrieve it.

The puppy ran briskly to the tavern and nudged his way through the swinging doors. The bartender noted his entrance and, pointing a long finger at him, demanded, "What'll you have?"

"Pap's blue ribbon," answered the pup.

* * *

The poodles were comparing unusual names and pedigrees. There were Henri, André, Suzette. A mongrel poodle said his name was Fido. "So what's so unusual about that?" he was asked. "Wait till you hear me spell it," he said, "P-H-I-D-E-A-U-X."

* * *

An actor met an honest-to-goodness bullfighter south of the border and asked him "How many bulls do you figure you've met?"

"At least two hundred, senor," smirked the bullfighter.

"You must be the envy of every cow in Mexico," marveled the actor.

SHOOTING A LEOPARD ON THE SPOT

The circus owner was dining peacefully one evening when a new circus employee burst into the room and cried, "One of the leopards has escaped. What'll we do?"

"Find him, and if you can't corner him, shoot him on the spot," ordered the circus owner.

An hour later the man returned and said, "I forgot to ask you; which spot?"

* * *

The man appeared at the agent's office and demanded an audition for his talking dog. "Okay," said the agent, "make him spell cat."

"K-A-T," said dog.

The agent hit the roof. "How the hell do you expect me to book him?" he roared. "He can't even spell cat!"

IF YOUR HORSE LIMPS

Client to veterinarian: "Something is wrong with my horse. One day it limps, and the next day it doesn't. What should I do?"

Veterinarian: "On the day it doesn't limp, sell it!"

THE COW MECHANIC

A veterinarian's car stalled on a country road. When he got out to look under the hood a cow strolled over and said: "Your trouble is probably with the carburetor."

Startled, the veterinarian ran to the nearest farmhouse and told the farmer what had happened.

"Was that a large cow with a brown spot over the left eye?" asked the farmer.

"Yes," replied the puzzled veterinarian.

"Well, don't pay any attention to her," drawled the farmer. "She doesn't know anything about cars."

ALL PASSENGERS ARE CREATED EQUAL

A woman with a dog was preparing to board a train. "I suppose," she said to the train conductor, "if I pay fare for my dog, he will be treated the same as other passengers and be allowed to occupy a seat."

"Of course, Madam," the conductor replied politely, "he will be treated the same as other passengers, and can occupy a seat, provided he does not put his feet on it."

ZEBRAS AND THE ARK

Two zebras were standing in the rain waiting to get into Noah's Ark. Says one: "It's enough to shake your faith when they insist on taking us alphabetically."

HE'LL HAVE ME HOLLERING "ICE"

Luigi and Vincente made a solemn pact that the one who died first would make every effort to make contact with the one left on earth. Luigi was the first to go, and for months Vincente waited in vain for a word or a sign.

Then, one day as he was walking down a side street, Vincente heard a soft voice: "Vincente, my friend! It's Luigi."

Vincente looked frantically in every direction, but the only living thing in sight was a spindly, underfed horse hitched to a dilapidated ice-wagon.

"Yeah," said the horse sadly, "it's me, Luigi! Live as long as you can, Vincente, for see what happens when you die! This pig Giuseppe who owns me beats me, starves me, and makes me lug this ice-wagon around sixteen hours a day!"

"But, Luigi," protested Vincente, "you can talk. Why don't you raise hell with Giuseppe."

"S-s-sh," cautioned Luigi. "For God's sake, don't let him know I can talk. He'll have me hollering 'Ice'!".

THE POKER-PLAYING DOG

In the card room of a social club, a member was surprised to see three men and a dog playing poker. He stopped to watch, and then commented on the extraordinary performance of the dog.

"He's not so smart," said the partner. "Every time he gets a good hand he wags his tail and gives it away."

LION TAMING, THE LOVING WAY

"Yes, I'm the man who advertised for a top-notch lion tamer," nodded the owner of a small-time carnival. "Are you applying for the job?"

The husky farmhand nodded once, patted the gun in his holster, picked up a chair and a whip, and said, "let me at him!"

"Not so fast," warned the owner, "there is one application ahead of yours. We'll have to give her first whack."

"Her?" echoed the farmhand incredulously.

"Yes, it's a girl," admitted the owner. "I, too, was surprised. Here she comes."

With that, a beautiful blonde burst upon the scene, draped in a full-length coat, but without the usual lion tamer's equipment—no gun, no whip, no chair.

"You're not going into the cage like that!" gasped the owner. "My lion is the meanest, most savage beast ever brought back alive."

"I don't scare easy," yawned the girl. "I've handled bulls; I can handle a lion."

With that, she unlocked the door and strode nonchalantly to the center of the lion's cage. There she flung open her fur coat. Underneath it, she was wearing nothing at all.

The lion's eyes bulged, gave out a deep M-G-M roar, and leaped at her. But there was no bloodshed. The lion swabbed his great red tongue across her cheek, gently kissed her hands and feet, licked her face again and again, and then climbed back on his stool in the corner!

The carnival owner shook his head unbelievingly and demanded of the farmhand, "Do you think you can do better than that?"

"Hell, yes," boasted the farmhand. "You get that damn lion out of there and I'll show you!"

THE THIEVING ELEPHANT

An elephant trainer was so down on his luck that he and his elephant were forced to take to a life of crime. The trainer would send the beast into a jewelry store, and in the resulting confusion the elephant would inhale mightily, sucking up thousands of dollars' worth of gems in his trunk. The elephant would then march out and rendezvous with the trainer to split the loot.

One day, one of the victims, after recovering from the initial shock, realized what had happened and called the police.

"I've been robbed by an elephant," cried the jeweler.

"Can you describe the thief?" asked the officer.

"Well, he was sort of elephant-looking: big and gray and wrinkled, with a long trunk."

"That's not much to go on. Can't you give me a better description?"

"What do you want? An elephant is an elephant."

"No. That's not exactly true. For instance, was the elephant who robbed you an Indian or an African elephant?"

"What's the difference?"

"An Indian elephant has small ears close to the head, and an African elephant has large, floppy ears. What kind of ears did this elephant have?"

"How should I know?" screeched the jeweler sarcastically. "He was wearing a stocking over his head."

* * *

At a bullfight in sunny Madrid
A tourist went clear off his lid.
He made straight for the bull
While the crowd yelled, "The fool
Will go home on a slab"—and he did.

A DOGGIE CALLED MOTHER

A friend of mine who had her hands full with four young children was taken aback when one day her husband came home with a young, frisky puppy. The children, all excited, asked the mother what they should name the pup.

"Better call it Mother," she said, "because if that dog stays, I'm going!"

* * *

Why did the three little pigs leave home?
Their father was such an awful boar.

ARE YOU PRAYING WID ME?

One Sunday, an old southern preacher, informed that a lion had broken loose from a nearby zoo, told the members of his congregation to have faith in God, and not be afraid of the lion if they should run into him on their way home.

"If you pray hard enough," he said, "you need not fear. The lion outside will not bodder you."

After services, the preacher himself was met by the lion. The preacher got down on his knees, and said, "Oh Lord! please hear my prayer. You saved Daniel from a lion, and I know you gonna save me from dis here lion." He raised his head after a while to see what the lion was doing. To his surprise, the lion was also kneeling with his paws clasped over his eyes.

"Brother lion, are you praying wid me?" he asked.

The lion looked up at him and replied, "No, brother, I'se saying mah grace befo' meals."

CITY BANKER & FARMER

"I suppose that's the hired man."

"Naw, that's the first vice president in charge of cows."

A FATAL BRAND NAME

A newly-settled rancher was asked by his neighbor the name of his spread.

"Our family had quite a time picking a name," he admitted, "so to please everyone, we call it the Lazy Rocker—Triple W—Diamond Bar—Lucky Sevens Ranch."

"Where are the cattle?" asked the nieghbor.

"There arent any," was the reply. "None of them survived the branding."

WHAT BEES THESE MORTAL FOOLS

A practical joker built a beehive with a false (painted on) entrance. He enjoyed watching bee after bee ram his head against the entrance and fall stunned.

One bee, however, wiser than the rest, did not fall for the trick. It stood aside, shaking its head at the goings-on.

"Why are you shaking your head, wise one?" a young bee asked.

"I am just thinking," replied the elder, "what bees these mortals fool."

COUNT THE TEATS AND DIVIDE BY FOUR

A rancher on a citybound train found the man next to him acting strangely: glancing quickly out of the window, muttering to himself, then glancing out of the window again. "Is there anything wrong?" he asked the stranger.

"No, indeed! I happen to be a lightning calculator, you see. And just for fun I count the number of cars parked in the street as we pass towns, the number of people waiting in train stations, the number of trees in a grove ... I never make a mistake."

"Wonderful," said the rancher. "In a few moments we're going to pass my farm. I know the exact number of cows grazing there. Would you care. . .?"

"Delighted!" responded the stranger, anxious to be put to the test.

As the train flashed past, he gave one quick glance toward the cows and announced, "157."

"Amazing," exclaimed the rancher. "How did you do it?"

"It's easy," replied the calculator. "All I did was to count the cows' teats and divide by four."

* * *

After her first horseback ride at the local ranch, a young lady was heard to make this comment: "I never imagined anything filled with hay could ride so hard."

FRESH FLESH

The steed bit his master;
    How come this to pass?
He heard the good pastor
    Cry, "All flesh is grass."

LAYING ODDS ON A PARROT

A Las Vegas bookmaker was given a parrot in lieu of cash by one of his clients. The bookmaker was thrilled when he discovered what a smart bird he had acquired. Not only did it speak English perfectly, but French and Spanish as well.

On night, the bookie took his bird with him to a casino and while standing at the bar, began to rave to the bartender about the parrot. Having heard such claims before, the bartender was not impressed. Irritated, the bookie offered to bet the bartender fifty dollars that his parrot could speak to him in three different languages. The bet was quickly made.

"Parlez-vous français?" said the bookie to the parrot. There was no response. Nor did the parrot respond to questions in English or Spanish, and the bartender pocketed the fifty dollars.

When they were outside, the bookie screamed at his bird, "What a stupid parrot you are! You just cost me fifty dollars! What's wrong with you?"

"Don't be a jerk," replied the parrot. "Just think of the odds you'll be able to get in that joint tomorrow!"

STRATEGIC PLANNING

A small boy looked longingly at a friend's dog. "My mother won't let me have a dog for Christmas," he said to a friend.

"Maybe you haven't used the right strategy," replied the friend.

"What strategy should I use?"

"Don't ask for a dog. Ask for a baby brother. *Then* you'll get the dog."

TURTLE TRUST

Once upon a time two large turtles and a little one went to a bar to quench their thirst with some sarsaparilla. As they began to drink it, one of the large turtles looked through the window and noticed that a heavy rain was falling. The turtles knew they would be drenched if they tried to leave, and it was decided that the little turtle should go home for an umbrella.

The little turtle demurred, afraid that if he went the big turtles would drink his sarsaparilla. But they convinced the little fellow that they would leave his mug alone, and he started after the umbrella.

An hour passed; a day passed; then a whole week. Fianlly, after three weeks, one of the big turtles said to the other, "Something must've happened. Let's drink the little guy's sarsaparilla."

"I've been thinking the same thing," said the other, "so let's do it."

From down at the end of the bar, right near the exit, a shrill voice cried: "If you do, I won't go!

* * *

As the woman turned on the lights, she screamed

and ran to the phone. "There's a rat in my room," she shrieked.

"Send him down at once!" ordered the room clerk. "He must register."

PEDIGREE CUM LAUDE

A woman purchasing a dog asked the kennel owner if the animal was pedigreed.

"Lady," answered the breeder, "if this dog could talk, he wouldn't speak to either one of us."

*   *   *

At the circus in Chicago last year, a man was observed near the camels. He picked up a straw, placed it squarely on a camel's back, and waited. Nothing happened. "Wrong straw," he muttered, and hurried off.

*   *   *

At a dog show in Boston, two matrons inspecting the various breeds asked a young attendant: "Can you direct us to the Labradors?"

"Yes, it's the second door on your right."

A DEAD CAT IN HEAVEN?

A little girl's cat was hit by a car and she rushed with it to the veterinary hospital. It was too late. The cat was dead on arrival.

Trying to comfort the child, the vet said, "Try to understand, honey, little Tabby has gone up to meet the Lord."

"Aw, c'mon, Doc," snapped the little girl. "What would God want with a dead cat?"

DOG SHOT

A veterinarian received a call about a hunting accident. "Is the dog shot bad?" he asked.

"Doc," answered the caller, "did you ever hear of a dog that was shot good?"

THE ONE I GOT AWAY FROM

On location, Raquel Welch took time off from her acting chores to go trout fishing. She hooked a whopper, but he finally broke loose and darted like all get-out to rejoin the other trout.

"Wow, fellows," he boasted, expanding his gills, "you should have seen the one I got away from!"

THE CHESS-PLAYING DOG

A man dropped in on a friend unexpectedly and was amazed to find him playing chess with his dog. The visitor watched in silence for a few moments, then screamed, "That's the most incredible dog I ever saw in my life!"

"Oh, he isn't so smart," replied his friend. I beat him three games out of four!"

A PIGEON STROLL

In Trafalgar Square lived a boy pigeon; at Saint Paul's a girl pigeon. One day as they were expressing the exuberance of youth by flying over London, they almost flew into each other. It was love at first sight. They courted happily, meeting every day.

One glorious morning in early May, they made a date to meet at eleven o'clock in Trafalgar Square.

Usually prompt, the girl pigeon had not arrived by 11:05, and the boy pigeon was becoming anxious. At 11:15, he began pacing along a balustrade. At 11:30, he flew over the Square, first this way, then that; but there was no sign of the girl pigeon. The poor fellow hardly knew what to do next.

Finally he decided to call the police and, just as he was about to ring Whitehall 1212 to ask whether any serious accident had been reported, he saw his little *amour* strolling gayly down the steps of the National Gallery. He rushed to meet her, and as he was about to tell her of the distress she had caused him, she chirped:

"Darling, I'm so sorry. Do forgive me, Georgie dear. But it was such a lovely morning I thought I'd walk."

A SLIPTH OF THE TONGUE

A copyreader on an Illinois newspaper couldn't believe it when he read a reporter's story about the theft of 2,025 pigs. "That's a lot of pigs," he growled, as he called the farmer to verify the report. "Is it true that you lost 2,025 pigs?"

"Yeth," lisped the farmer.

"Thanks," retorted the wise copyreader and corrected the copy to read, "two sows and 25 pigs."

WORRYING ABOUT THE WRONG THING

Two elderly ladies checked into a new hotel in Miami Beach that catered to a fast crowd. The first thing they noticed was a little man circulating from guest to guest in the lobby, whispering, and collecting money.

"What's he doing?" they asked.

"He's a bookie," was the answer. "He takes bets on horses."

Impulsively they decided to risk two dollars, and they lost.

One of the ladies was very upset, and was unable to sleep that night. In the morning her companion said, "Don't cry over spilt milk. Stop worrying. Your only lost two dollars!"

"I ain't worried about the two dollars. I was worried about winning. What would we have done with the horse?"

FIRED BY PELLETS

A Texan entered his thoroughbred in the famous race at Ascot, England. Just before the event, he slipped the horse a white pellet. The Duke of Marlboro, a steward at Ascot, caught the Texan in the act and said, "I say, old man, you can't do that sort of thing over here."

"Nothing but a lump of sugar," answered the Texan, whereupon he took a pellet from his pocket and swallowed it to prove his point. Then he took out another pellet and handed it to the duke. "Here, you have one."

The duke swallowed it, and seemed satisfied. As the starter lined up the field for the big race, the Texan whispered to his jockey, "Son, keep the horse on the outside once he's off. Nothing can catch him but me and the Duke of Marlboro."

TO GEESE A GANDER

Asked to write a composition about geese, this is what Bill turned in:

Geese is a low, heavy-set bird which is mostly meat and feathers. Geese can't sing much on account of the dampness of the moisture. He ain't got no between-the-toes and he's got a little balloon in his stummick to keep from sinking. Some geese when they get big has curls on their tails and is called ganders. Ganders don't haff to sit and hatch, but just eat and loaf and go swimming. If I was a geese, I'd rather be a gander.

ANIMAL CRACKS

Owl to baby owl: "How many times must I tell you? It's whooo, not whoom."

* * *

A youth was advising his friend what to look for at the zoo:

"There'll be a sign TO THE TIGERS—you'll like them; and another sign, TO THE GIRAFFES, and they're very interesting. But don't pay attention to the sign TO THE EXIT. I've looked; and there's nothing there."

* * *

A notice at Chicago's Lincoln Park Zoo advises: CLAIM LOST CHILDREN AT LION HOUSE. Someone added: BEFORE 4 PM FEEDING.

IT'S YOUR CHOICE, BESSIE

Carrying a milk pail, farmer Jones approaches a cow: "Well, Bessie, what will it be: milk or hamburger?"

FIFTY CENTS FOR TRUNKS

A department store in San Francisco hired a taxi to drive a baby elephant to the city's zoo. The elephant sat in the back seat.

At the end of the ride, the driver tried to collect an extra fifty cents on the fare.

"We're allowed that extra charge," argued the cabbie "whenever we carry a trunk."

LADY UNCLES

A schoolteacher asked the pupils to write a short essay and to choose their own subjects.

A little girl sent in the following paper:

My subject is "Ants." Ants is of two kinds, insects and lady uncles. Sometimes they live in holes, and sometimes they crawl into the sugar bole, and sometimes they live with their married sisters. That's all I know about ants.

A FLYING STOIC

"Now can anyone tell me what a stoic is?" asked the teacher of the fourth grade.

Abraham raised his hand. "Very well, Abraham."

"A stoic," he replied, "is a boid what brings de babies."

SILENT SAM

"Now, children," said the teacher, "I want each of you to think of some animal or bird. Now, try, for the moment, to be like the particular one you are thinking about, and make the same kind of noises they are in the habit of making."

Instantly the room became a menagerie: Lions roaring, dogs barking, birds singing and twittering, cows lowing, calves bleating, cats meowing, etc. Every child carried on excitedly—all except one little boy who was off in a corner sitting perfectly still, unmindful of all the turmoil.

"Sam, why are you not taking part with the other children?" asked the teacher.

Sam waved her off, whispering, "Sh-sh-sh, teacher! I'm a rooster and I'm laying an egg."

POLY-EUPHEMISM

Mathematics teacher: "Robert, can you tell me what is meant by a polygon?"

Robert (a freshman): "I guess it means a parrot that's died, doesn't it?"

JIMMY DURANTE ON HORSES

Jimmy Durante bet on a horse at Santa Anita that lost by inches.

"What that horse needed," bragged an ex-jockey, "was my riding."

"What he needed," corrected Durante, "was my nose."

A BEAR HUG

"Grandpa, tell me again about the Three Bears," begged little Sammy.

"Ah, you don't want to hear that old story again," protested Grandpa. "Better I'll tell you about the One Bear."

"Ooh, goodie!"

"Well, when I was a young fellow in Russia, I would sometimes go to Siberia to hunt grizzly bears. One day, I was walking through the frozen tundra when suddenly, right in front of my nose, a tremendous female bear rose up before me. I quickly aimed my gun and pulled the trigger. No bullets! I was just about to turn and run when, all at once, she threw her arms around me and began to squeeze and hug me.

Sammy's eyes were wide with excitement. "What did you do, Grandpa?"

"What could I do?" demanded Grandpa. "I kissed her!"

A HORSE AT THE BAR

A horse walked up to a bar and asked for a martini with catsup. "Okay, bud," said the bartender, and mixed it pronto. After tossing off the drink with considerable and obvious relish, the horse leaned over the bar and said:

"I suppose you think it is strange that a horse should come in and ask for a martini with catsup in it."

"Hell, no," said the bartender. "I like them that way myself."

SHEEP HEAVEN

A little boy whose pet sheep had died recently was somewhat consoled after visiting a cemetery one Sunday afternoon.

"Mama," said the boy as he noticed quite a few marble figures of lambs on the tombstones, "I guess I ain't the only one that's lost a sheep. There seems to be a lot of 'em buried here."

THE BULL IN ELMER

A little girl answered a knock on the door of the farmhouse. The caller, a rather troubled-looking middleaged man, asked to see her father.

"If you come about the bull," she said, "he's fifty dollars. We have the papers and everything and he's guaranteed."

"Young lady," the man said, "I want to see your father."

"If that's too much," the little girl replied, "we got another bull for twenty-five dollars, and he's guaranteed, too, but he doesn't have any papers."

"Young lady," the man repeated, "I want to see your father!"

"If that's too much," said the little girl, "we got

another bull for ten dollars, but he's not guaranteed."

"I'm not here for a bull," said the man angrily. "I want to talk about your brother, Elmer. He's gotten my daughter in trouble!"

"Oh, I'm sorry," said the little girl. "You'll have to see Pa about that 'cause I don't know what he charges for Elmer."

WELL-SEASONED PHOTOGRAPHERS

Two seasoned photographers were sent to Alaska to film the wildlife of America's last great wilderness. One day, they encountered a grizzly bear catching salmon by a quiet stream. The huge beast spotted them and stood up on his hind legs striking a magnificent pose. The photographers excitedly reached for their cameras when, suddenly, the bear charged. But the two kept right on shooting pictures of the grizzly as he closed the distance between them.

Finally, one of the men said nervously, "Joe, there are no trees tall enough to climb around here. What in the name of heaven are we going to do?"

"I'm not sure," his friend replied anxiously. "But one of us is going to get one hell of a picture!"

MICE DON'T LIKE FLOUNDER

"Doctor, Doctor," called Mr. Schultz frantically, "come quick. My wife always sleeps with her mouth wide open and just now a mouse ran down her throat."

"I'll be right over," said the doctor, "but meanwhile, try waving a piece of cheese in front of her mouth. Maybe the mouse will come out."

When the doctor reached the Schultz apartment, he found Mr. Schultz in his shirt sleeves frantically waving a six-pound flounder in front of prostrate Mrs. Schultz's face.

"What's the idea," asked the exasperated doctor. "I told you to wave a piece of cheese. Don't you know mice don't like flounder."

"I know, I know," screamed Mr. Schultz, "but we've got to get the cat out first."

SPOT'S PEDIGREE

"How did you get your dog Spot?" a little boy was asked.

"I got Spot because my parents gave him to me because I made my bed every day this last summer.

"What kind of dog is Spot?" the little boy was then asked.

"Spot is dark brown, with white patches. He has short furry legs, and one ear is flopped over. He has a very small tail and he is a son of a bitch."

PLANTINGS THAT WON'T GROW

A boy was watching his dad filling in the grave of a cat that had just been hit by a car. "Dad, it won't do no good," he said. "It won't grow."

PRAY & PREY

Behold the mantis,
  Solemn creature,
Arms uplifted
  Like a preacher!

'Tis a reverent
  Attitude
Not for worship,
  But for food.

Artless insects,
  Venturing near,
In his gullet
  Disappear.

Mark the moral:
  Be ye ware!
All that's ritual
  Is not prayer.

Some be pious
  For display,
And, like the mantis
  Pray . . . and prey!

HORSE AT BAT

A baseball scout found a remarkable prospect: a horse who was not only a pretty good fielder, but could hit the ball every time he was at bat.

The first time up with his new team, the horse slammed the ball into far left field and just stood there at the plate.

"Run!" the manager screamed.

"Are you kidding?" said the horse, "If I could run, I'd be at the track."

A "UNANIMOUS" LETTER

Old Mose received an anonymous letter one day that contained a single sentence: "If you don't stop stealing my chickens, I'm gonna cut out your gizzard."

Mose was so bothered that he consulted the local constable. The peace officer listened to the complaint, then laughed and said, "Well, all you've got to do is stop stealing the chickens."

"You don' seem to understand, constable," said Mose. "Dis letter am 'unanimous.' Whose chickens is I supposed to stop stealin'?"

A FINNISH SPECIALTY

A married couple returning by steamer to the United States after a trip to Finland noticed an attractive, red-cheeked Finnish girl in steerage. They learned that she was coming to America to look for work, and decided to offer her employment.

"Can you cook?" they asked.

"No," said the girl, "I can't cook. My mother always did the cooking."

"Well, then you can do housework?"

"No," she answered, "my oldest sister always did the housework."

"Well, then, we could let you take care of the children."

"No, I couldn't do that. My youngest sister always took care of the children."

"Then, can you sew?"

"No," said the girl, "my aunt always did the sewing."

"What *can* you do?" cried the despairing couple.

"I can milk reindeer!" replied the girl triumphantly.

BULL/WORK

A tourist on a country road watched a little girl leading a cow.

"Little girl," he asked, "where are you taking that cow?"

"To the bull," she said.

"Can't your father do it?" he asked.

"Nope," she replied, "only the bull."

* * *

Vet Student: "Do animals with this condition die very often?"

Professor: "No. Only once."

COWARD! COWARD!

A Yankee farmer and his wife visited the zoo. At the hippopotamus cage, the farmer stopped to admire the huge animal. "Durned curi's fish, ain't it, ma?"

"That ain't a fish," his wife announced. "That's a rep-tile."

"No, it ain't!" countered the farmer. Thus the argument began, and then progressed to a point of such intensity that the old lady began belaboring her husband with her umbrella. The old man dodged and ran, with his wife in hot pursuit.

As he raced by the lion's cage, the trainer had just opened the door of the cage, and the farmer scrambled in and crawled behind the largest lion.

The farmer's wife caught up with him and from the other side of the bars, shook her umbrella furiously and shouted, Coward! Coward!"

BEDBUG SNOOPS

Just as the traveler was writing his name in the hotel register, a bedbug appeared and walked across the page. Said the surprised traveler: "I'll be darned if I was ever in a place where the bedbugs looked over the hotel register to find out where your room was."

SHEEP TALK

Two sheep were grazing in a meadow. "Baa-aa-aaa," said the first sheep.

"Moooo," said the second sheep.

"What do you mean, Moooo?" asked the first sheep.

"I'm studying a foreign language," was the reply.

THE DOG AND THE PARROT

A dog and a parrot were brought into a bar one day by a regular customer who, having ordered his drink, turned to the dog and said, "*Now,* fella!"

At that point the dog started a lively conversation with the bird. When the conversation ended, one of the other customers turned to the owner of the remarkable creatures and said, "That's really something! A dog and parrot that can converse!"

"Well, it's not as great as you think."

"How's that?" asked the customer.

Moving closer to the customer the pet owner whispered, "The dog is a ventriloquist."

BEWARE OF INCEST

A woman called the veterinarian to administer to her sick cat. The animal doctor examined the cat and told the woman the cat was expecting.

"That's impossible," said the woman. "She hasn't been near a male cat."

Just then a bit tomcat strolled into the room. "How about him?" asked the doctor.

"Don't be silly," said the woman, "that's her brother."

MY WIFE KNOWS BEST

A man called his veterinarian to complain about a swelling on his dog's leg and was instructed by the doctor to apply heat to the leg.

"But, doctor," objected the client, "my wife says cold packs are better for swelling."

"You tell your wife," answered the vet, "my wife thinks heat is best!"

EATING IN BED

A kangaroo yanked her young one out of her pouch and gave it a healthy smack on the backside.

"That'll teach you to eat crackers in bed!"

FOOTBALL ON THE ARK

During the forty days and forty nights on Noah's Ark, time was hanging heavy, and the animals were getting jittery. So the tiger suggested to the giraffe that they choose sides for a football game. The giraffe agreed. The tiger's team kicked off, and on the first play from scrimmage, the monkey handed off to the rhino, who charged up the middle for ten yards. On the next play, the rhino rumbled its way through the defensive team for a touchdown. At half time the giraffe's team was leading 42-0.

Early in the second half, the monkey again handed off to the rhino. The rhino headed for a hole in the line, but the centipede, who was playing defensive tackle, dug in and grabbed the rhino, throwing him to the deck, and causing a fumble. The rabbit, who was playing free safety, picked up the ball and scored for the tiger's team. The tiger was elated.

"Fantastic tackle!" shouted the tiger to the centipede. "Where were you in the first half?"

"I was lacing my shoes," replied the centipede.

FORD'S GOLDEN PET

President Ford once told a Republican rally in South Dakota how he got his dog Liberty. His daughter, Susan, it seems, called a highly recommended kennel and said she wanted a golden retriever.

"Fine," said the kennel operator. "And what will the owner's name be?"

"It's a surprise," said Susan. "I can't tell you."

"We don't sell animals that way," said the operator. "We must be sure the animal will be placed in a good home."

"Don't worry," said Susan. "The dog will have a good home."

Then she explained that the dog was for her parents, and that they are friendly, middleaged people who live in a white house with a fence all around it.

"Good," said the operator. "Do they own it or rent?"

"You might say, it's public housing," answered Susan.

THE MASTER WHIP LASHER

One day Ananias, the tall, black coachman of the Kaufman estate was driving his master down a long lane on the way to a neighboring plantation, when a horsefly alighted on the mane of one of the horses.

"Massa," said Ananias, "yuh see dat hossfly on dat hoss's mane? Watch me git 'im."

Ananias had the reputation of being the most exact wielder of the coachwhip in the county, and his master always enjoyed watching him crack it. Ananias raised his whip and split the horsefly into two neat parts.

A little further down the lane Ananias looked over and spied a centipede crawling on a flower. "Massa," said Ananias, "yuh see dat crawler on dat flower? Watch me git 'im." Ananias raised his whip again and the centipede was torn to shreds at the snap of the lash.

After a little while the master noticed a beehive hanging from the limb of a tree by the side of the road. "Look, Ananias," said he. "You see that beehive? You are such an expert with the coachwhip, let me see you cut that hive off the limb."

"No, sah, Massa," stammered Ananias. "Ah ain't gwine bothah dem bees. Dey's auganized!"

THE NOISY CENTIPEDE

One night, just before retiring, the elephant on Noah's Ark started to scream at the top of his voice. Noah ran downstairs.

"What's the matter?" asked Noah.

"I can't sleep," said the elephant, "there's too much noise upstairs!"

Noah ran upstairs to see what was happening. He soon returned and announced: "You must have a little patience, please, the centipede is taking his shoes off."

AMISH DISCIPLINE

Several years ago, an Amish father caught his two boys in a local tavern having a beer. The disapproving father promptly disciplined his sons. "I'll take the horse home," he told them. "You boys bring the buggy!"

THE FOURTH "R"

A cotton-tail rabbit, nibbling thoughtfully on his evening carrot, noticed that his son was in a particularly jovial mood.

"What makes junior so happy?" he asked mama rabbit.

"He had a wonderful time in school today. He learned how to multiply," explained mama.

FLAT CAT

A veterinarian was performing a routine examination on a champion Abyssinian cat when it escaped through a window and was run over by a steamroller. Reports of the incident stated the doctor neither spoke nor cried as he picked up the remains; he just stood there with a long puss.

ERASING LIONS

A man reputed to have psychological problems was making some rather peculiar motions.

"Why are you doing that?" the psychiatrist asked.

"To keep lions away," he said.

"But there are no lions within thousands of miles!" responded the doctor.

"See how effective it is!" he replied.

PITY THE BLIND

A well-known Edinburgh beggar was often seen plodding along the street with a small dog. Around the dog's neck was a placard on which was printed, in large red letters: PITY THE BLIND.

A gentleman, passing one day, dropped a sixpence into the beggar's outstretched cup. "Hey there," he cried, as he was turning away, "was that a half-sovereign I gave to you?"

"Nae, nae," answered the beggar, "only a sixpence."

"So," said the gentleman, "you're not blind after all?"

"Bless ye, nae," the beggar replied. " 'Tis the dog that's blind, no' me."

AND WHAT DO YOU DO?

A zebra that had been performing for a circus took ill and the local veterinarian prescribed a few weeks rest for the beast. Arrangements were made to board it at a local farm.

The zebra took to the new life well, and spent the first day meeting all the animals of the barnyard.

First, he met a chicken and said, "I'm a zebra, who are you?"

"I'm a chicken," said the chicken.

"What do you do?" asked the zebra.

"I scratch around and lay eggs," said the chicken.

Moving on, the zebra found a cow. He introduced himself saying, "I'm a zebra. Who are you?"

"I'm a cow," said the cow.

"What do you do?" asked the zebra.

"I graze in the field and give milk," said the cow.

The zebra met a bull next. "I'm a zebra," he said. "Who are you?"

"I'm a bull," said the bull.

"And what do you do?" asked the zebra.

"What do I do!" snorted the bull, pawing at the turf with a forefoot. "Why you silly-looking ass — take off your pajamas and I'll show you."

A MOST CONVINCING LAWYER

A man in North Carolina who had been acquitted of the charge of stealing through the powerful plea of his lawyer, was asked by his lawyer:

"Bill, you *did* steal that horse, didn't you?"

"I allers did think I stole that hoss, but since I heard your speech to that 'ere jury, I'll be doggoned if I a'n't got my doubts about it."

THE LADDER OF LOGIC

A fat old gentleman was bitten in the calf of his leg by a dog. He at once rushed to the office of the justice of the peace and preferred a complaint against a joker in the neighborhood, whom he supposed to be the owner of the offending cur. The following was the defense offered at the trial by the alleged owner:

> First, by testimony in favor of the general good character of my dog, I shall prove that nothing could make him so forgetful of his canine dignity as to bite a *calf.* Second, he is blind and cannot see to bite. Third, even if he could see to bite, it would be utterly impossible for him to go out of his way to do so, on account of his severe lameness. Fourth, granting his eyes and legs to be good, he has no teeth. Fifth, my dog died six weeks ago. Sixth, I never had a dog!

A MYNAH OFFENSE

An owner, who spent his spare time teaching his new little bird to say dirty words, was recently arrested for contributing to the delinquency of a mynah.

RELIGIOUS PENGUINS

A mother lost her young daughter at the railroad station. After a frantic search, she finally located her in the midst of a group of nuns. The little girl and the nuns seemed to be having a great time.

"I hope my daughter hasn't been giving you too much trouble," said the relieved parent.

"On the contrary," chuckled the Mother Superior. "Your little girl seems to have the notion that we are penguins."

A MILD COMPROMISE

Harry and Joe were old friends who loved to brag about their fishing accomplishments, each trying to outdo the other.

"Did I catch a herring!" Harry boasted. "I'm telling you, it was the biggest herring ever seen by mortal man. It weighed 500 pounds, if it weighed an ounce."

"That's nothing, Harry," smirked Joe. "Last

week as I pulled up my line, do you know what I found on my hook? Nothing less than a ship's lamp. I should live so long! And not only that, it had a date engraved on the bottom: 1392; a hundred years before Columbus came to America. And that's not all. Inside the lamp was a light, and it was still burning."

Harry studied his friend's face for a moment and then he grinned. "Listen, Joe, let's compromise. I'll knock 495 pounds off the herring if you'll blow out the light."

* * *

A pair of rabbits were being chased by a pack of hounds, when one said, "What are we running for? Let's stop and outnumber them."

"Keep running, you idiot," replied the other. "We're brothers!"

* * *

The trouble with a husband who works like a horse is that all he wants to do evenings is hit the hay.

A VERY RELIGIOUS HORSE

A man owned a remarkable horse which would go only if the rider said, "Praise the Lord," and it would stop only if he said, "Amen."

One day, the owner decided to sell the horse, but when he explained the horse's peculiarities to a prospective buyer, the buyer said, "That's ridiculous. I've been raising horses all my life. I'll make him go *my* way."

So the new owner jumped on the horse and proceeded to kick him until he started to run. The horse went faster and faster. Worried, the new owner reined back and yelled, "Whoa!" But the horse wouldn't stop.

Suddenly, the man saw they were galloping toward the edge of a cliff, and in desperation shouted, "Oh, all right, *Amen!*"

The horse screeched to a halt just in time. Peering down the edge of the cliff, the perspiring owner wiped his brow and said, "Wow, that was close. Praise the Lord!"

THE SOUL OF A DOG

An attorney came to a minister to ask him to officiate at the funeral of Shep, a client's dog.

"But dogs don't have souls," protested the clergyman.

"That may be," said the lawyer, "but five hundred dollars was left in the will of the owner for the burial of his dog."

The preacher shifted gears quickly. "Why didn't you tell me that Old Shep was a Baptist?"

CANINE SERVICE

A very rich lady had a dog who had his own little doghouse complete with little furniture. A neighbor was looking at it one day and asked, "How does he keep it so clean?"

The owner said haughtily, "Oh, he has a French poodle come in once a week."

FLEA COLLECTION

"My aunt collects fleas for a living."
"What does your uncle do?"
"Scratches himself."

BABY BEAR'S CACTUS

Papa Bear, Mama Bear, and Baby Bear, treking through the Nevada desert, decided to rest. Unknowingly, Papa Bear sat down on a piece of cactus, and quickly jumped to his feet, hollering "Ouch."

Mama Bear likewise sat on a piece of cactus, and jumped up screaming at the top of her voice.

Baby Bear, however, squatted on the same type of cactus and remained there unperturbed.

Papa Bear watched him with growing concern and then turned to Mama Bear and said, "Mama, don't tell me we're raising one of those Dead-End Kids!"

ALLIGATOR TEETH

A veterinarian admired his receptionist's beads and asked what they were made of.

"Alligator teeth," replied the receptionist. "They're more valuable than pearls."

"Why?" asked the veterinarian.

"Because anyone can open an oyster."

INDIAN SIGNS

A cowboy riding across the prairie came upon an Indian lying on the ground with his ear glued to a wagon track.

Said the Indian: "Wagon. Two horses—one white, one black. Man drive, smoke pipe. Woman have blue dress, wear bonnet."

"You mean you can tell that by listening to the ground?" asked his cowboy friend.

"No," said the Indian. "They run over me, half hour ago."

HOOKED SUMMER CLIENTS

Our local veterinarian, known for his wry humor, outdid himself one summer day when a city dog was brought in after an encounter with a porcupine. After an hour of prying, pulling, cutting, and stitching, he returned the dog to its owner, who asked how much she owed for the visit.

"Fifteen dollars, ma'am," said the vet.

"Why, that's simply outrageous!" she stormed. "That's what's wrong with you Maine people, you're always trying to overcharge summer visitors. Whatever do you do in the winter, when we're not here to be gypped?"

"Raise porcupines, ma'am."

A WORD TO THE DUMB

The next time you call your dog a dumb animal, remember who's working to support him.

* * *

Sign in veterinarian's office:
WILL BE BACK SHORTLY. SIT! STAY!

IT'S A WESTINGHOUSE

Charlie opened the family refrigerator and found his dog sitting inside.

"What are you doing there?" he asked.

"This is a Westingouse, isn't it?"

"So what of it?" said Charlie.

"Well, I'm westing."

HAIRY, BUT NOT ALL OVER

The hairy ape, now, chillun see,
He's lookin' fo' a li'l ole flea.
If he should tuhn aroun' we'd fine
He has no hair on his behine.

HOW DO LIONS MAKE LOVE?

While visiting the zoo with her mother, a little girl asked, "Mommy, how do lions make love?"

"I don't know dear," replied the mother. "Most of your father's friends are Rotarians."

THE TALKING DOG NO ONE BELIEVED

Once there was a man who claimed his dog could talk, and he entered him in a talent show. Onstage, the man asked the dog, "What is the outside of a tree called?"

"Bark! Bark!" said the dog.

The audience booed.

"Well, what is found on the top of a house?" asked the man.

"Roof! Roof!" replied the dog.

The audience pelted him with tomatoes.

"What is the texture of sandpaper?" was the man's next question.

"Ruff! Ruff!" answered the dog, and the audience began to rush the stage.

In desperation, the man shouted out his final question: "Who was the greatest Yankee baseball player?"

"Ruth! Ruth!" barked the dog, and with that the audience chased them out of the theater.

Outside, the dog turned to his master and asked with a bewildered look, "DiMaggio?"

* * *

Tomcat: "I could die for you."
Tabby Cat: "Yeah! How many times?"

A NO-WAG DOG

A small animal practitioner was asked to crop the tail of a young dog so close that none of it would be visible. When asked the reason for this unusual request, the client replied, "My mother-in-law is coming for a visit and I want nothing in the house to be demonstrating joy."

THE ELEPHANT AND THE MOUSE

A huge elephant and a tiny mouse were in the same cage at the zoo. The elephant was in a particularly ugly mood. Looking down at the tiny mouse with disgust, he trumpeted, "You're the puniest, weakest, most insignificant thing I've ever seen!"

"Well," piped the mouse in a plaintive squeak, "don't forget, I've been sick."

HOT ON THE TRAIL

A Californian, on the trail of a grizzly bear for three days, returned without his game.

"Lost the trail, Bill, I suppose," said one of his cronies.

"Naw, I kept on the trail all right."

"Then what's the matter?"

"The footprints was getting too fresh for me."

*   *   *

I caught a fish so big I got up in the middle of the night and called myself a liar.

*   *   *

Note to hunters: If it stands on its hind legs, and has a pipe in its mouth, it isn't a squirrel.

A SUCCESSFUL BEE YEAR

"Have your bees done well this year?" asked the honey buyer.

"Well, they haven't given much honey," said the breeder, "but they stung my mother-in-law."

DEER TO DEER

One deer to a brother deer: "Man, I wish I had his doe."

DOWN BOY

A city dog met a country dog.

"What's your name?" inquired the country dog.

"I'm not quite sure," admitted the city dog, "but I think it's Down Boy."

DUCKS DON'T SINK

A motorist in Louisiana found the bridge over a stream washed away by a recent storm. A native sat whittling a stick by the side of the wreckage.

"How deep is this stream?" asked the motorist.

"Dunno."

"Think I can drive through it?"

"Sure thing. Why not?"

The emboldened motorist drove head-on into the stream. His car promptly sank out of sight, and he himself barely got out with his life.

"What do you mean by telling me I could drive through that stream?" the dripping motorist cried furiously. "Why, it's ten feet deep if it's an inch!"

The native scratched his head. "Can't understand it," he said pointing to his chest. "The water's only up to *there* on the ducks."

TEA FOR LIONS

English writer Alec Waugh tells about the little girl who visited a zoo and was fascinated to see the keepers tossing food to the animals. Later, in a composition she wrote, "We were very lucky to get there in the afternoon just when the lions were having tea."

HUMBLE BUMBLEBEES

Why do bumblebees hum?
Because they don't know the words.

PULLING THE WOOL

A sheepdog at Provincetown fell insanely in love with another sheepdog. Into her ear one night at the kennel door, he whispered, "Mary, I cannot live another day without you. . . . You are Mary, aren't you?"

* * *

A newborn calf approached a silo and asked sadly, "Is my fodder in dere?"

* * *

"It won't take long—did it?" said the male rabbit to his bride.

SWEET TWEET

There was the devil to pay when the singing canary fell into the meat grinder. All week the family ate nothing but shredded tweet.

A DOLLAR A BITE

A gorilla walked into Goldman's delicatessen and ordered a pastrami sandwich on pumpernickel with a piece of pickle on the side—to go.

"That'll be five dollars," said Goldman, handing the ape the sandwich. "And I must say, I never expected to see a gorilla in my store!"

"At five dollars a sandwich," snapped the gorilla, "you never will again!"

THE LAND OF THE BARK

Three dogs: an English bulldog, a French poodle, and a Russian wolfhound were talking. The English bulldog and the French poodle agreed that they loved their respective countries and were content to stay there. The Russian wolfhound said, "I have the best of everything to eat and drink in Russia, but I sure would like to go to America."

"How come?" asked the other two dogs.

"Well," said the wolfhound, "I'd like to know what it feels like to bark."

GETTING DOWN TO BASICS

Young boy to father: "If you didn't plan on buying me a dog, why did you ever have me in the first place?"

* * *

The doting mother asked her child, "Why are you making faces at the bulldog?"

"He started it," said the child.

MOTHER-DAUGHTER TALK

Mama rabbit to her daughter: "At your age I was already married and the mother of 138 children."

Ad in *Newburgh (N.Y.) News:*
> LOST—Gray mother cat. Will finder telephone 1705. Kittens miss their mother.

THE PERFECT HORSE

The Reverend Henry Ward Beecher needed a horse. The owner of the stable pointed to one and recommended it highly.

"Now here's one that is gentle and well-behaved. Stands anywhere without hitching. Does anything you ask him. Hasn't got a bad trait. Won't kick. Listens carefully to everything you say."

"Ah," said Beecher wistfully, "if that horse were only a member of my congregation."

* * *

A prudish, tight-lipped old maid never allowed her cat out of the house after dark. Headed for New York on one of her infrequent outings, she paused to remind the maid about locking up the cat each evening.

This time in New York, however, the old maid encountered a handsome old rogue who swept her off her feet. After four nights of blissful romanc-ing, she wired her maid: "Having the time of my life. *Let the cat out.*"

STAY AWAY FROM NAUGHTY WOMEN

Two thieving peasants, Boris and Ivan, saw a Jewish wagoner hitch his horse and car outside a tavern and then go inside.

"That's a fine-looking horse," said Boris greedily. "Young and strong."

"Let's steal it," said Ivan promptly.

"It's a litle risky," said Boris. "The Jew will be coming out in a minute or two. If we're caught, it's a good ten years in prison for us.

"But I have an idea," continued Boris. "We'll

→

unhitch the horse, and you ride him out of town to our hideout, as fast as you can. Meanwhile, I'll get into the harness myself."

When the wagoner came out of the tavern and saw a human being hitched to his wagon he was dumbfounded. "What happened to my horse?" he shrieked. "What are you doing here?"

"Hush! Don't carry on so!" soothed the stranger. "I *am* your horse. Many years ago, when I was a young man, I could not stay away from loose women, and so, for my transgressions the Lord punished me by changing me into a horse for eighteen years. My term just expired a few minutes ago and now I am a human being again."

The Jewish wagoner was full of compassion. "Oh, my dear man," he sighed, "when I think of all the times I treated you harshly, I could weep. I made you stand outside in the rain and snow. I loaded the wagon with more than you were able to pull. I didn't feed you as well as I should have. Tell me, my friend, how can I make it up to you?"

"Well, I'll need a little money to get started again as a human being," said Boris.

"Here's fifty rubles. Go your way, old friend, and stay away from naughty ladies."

On the following Tuesday, the Jewish driver went to the marketplace to buy a new horse, and lo and behold! There, tethered to a post, was his good old horse, up for sale.

The wagoner rushed over to the animal and threw his arms around his neck. "You old rascal," he whispered affectionately. "You transgressed again! I *told* you to stay away from naughty women."

* * *

Newspaper Ad: Bulldog for sale; will eat anything; is very fond of children.

* * *

Sign on a local milk truck: "From moo to you in an hour or two."

ABOUT THE AUTHORS

Murray Loring was awarded a Doctor of Veterinary Medicine degree by Middlesex University in 1944, and in 1968 earned a law degree from the College of William and Mary. He has conducted a private veterinary practice as well as a private law practice and is currently a consultant in animal law. Dr. Loring is the author of numerous published articles and of four published books. He and his wife, Mildred, reside in Williamsburg, Virginia.

*

Seymour Glasofer received his Doctor of Veterinary Medicine degree from Middlesex University in 1943. Since 1945 he has conducted a private veterinary practice in Newport News, Virginia, where he and his wife, Lillian, presently reside. Dr. Glasofer is the author of hundreds of animal-related articles and of *In Sickness and in Love* (1980), which recounts his veterinary career.

ABOUT THE ARTIST

Alex Bloch is a Soviet Union-trained commercial artist. He is a graduate of College of Scenic Art of Moscow (1964) and of the Institute of Printing Art of Moscow (1969). Currently, Mr. Bloch lives in New York City with his wife, Lucia.